GAMECH
for
WOMEN

Vol 1

CAREER DEVELOPMENT FOR WOMEN WITH AMBITION

LAURA TRENDALL

Cover image by: Alex_82, 99Designs
Book design by: SWATT Books Ltd

Printed in the United Kingdom
First Printing, 2023

ISBN: 978-1-915935-00-7 (Paperback)
ISBN: 978-1-915935-01-4 (eBook)

GameChanger Publishing
London WC2H 9JQ

www.gamechanger.vip

Contents

Section 2: Personal Brand   69

Section 3: Creating Your Powerful Network   103

Section 4: Action and Accountability   135

LAURA TRENDALL

Introduction

'm so pleased you have this book in your hands – this is designed to be the first volume in a series of *GameChanger for Women* books, and it has been inspired by my coaching work with women in business over the last 25 years.

I have now coached hundreds of women, just like you, who are looking for that next step, the next promotion, or the next level up in business.

This book is for women just like you. We deal with many different roles as women and I have helped many along the way to figure out how to navigate those roles to be successful, both personally and professionally.

We are women who want more. More freedom, more joy, more fulfilment, and to make a bigger impact whilst building business and profile, without sacrificing personal wellbeing, family and friends. The women that I work with are smart, inquisitive, willing to try new things and they are committed to striving to be their best. These are the women who are prepared to put the work in to get results.

The good news is that women in business today can achieve anything that they want.

However, to get there, you do need to put in the dedication and the time, to work on creating a firm foundation of the right knowledge, skills and attitude to ensure success.

GameChanger for Women is designed to help you set your direction and check those foundations. With this groundwork in place, you will be able to work in a way where you can achieve a successful and sustainable career path.

If you are looking for a book that is going to tell you the secrets of the universe and how to get rich quick, this is *not* the book you are looking for.

If you *are* looking for a grounded and practical approach to business and career planning, you are exactly where you should be. Even better than that, you can now be part of the international GameChanger for Women community: women, who are committed to achieving more, and who will grow and do great things in the future.

So, if you want to create your own plan to power up your productivity and change the game in your life and career, you are in **exactly the right place**!

I was inspired to write this book after reviewing my interviews and notes from mentoring and coaching senior women since 2008. I used my observations and findings to create the first GameChanger for Women Programme in 2016. I have also examined my own personal development journey and the practices that I have honed over 25 years in business, to pin down exactly **what** makes the difference and gives **GameChanger Women** the edge.

Right now, after the world events of 2020 and the uncertainty since, you probably find yourself ready for your next phase – what we thought we knew as certainty has changed beyond recognition, and well-laid plans are now cast to the winds. Yet this brings us the opportunity for change, growth, and renewal – to examine our lives and purpose with fresh eyes and look at new horizons, new opportunities, and to check we are living a fully aligned life that honours the values that matter to us. My hope as you read this book is that you are inspired to play your own bigger game, by your own rules.

My great passion is to help others and share knowledge to give people opportunities to grow, and for businesses to thrive, and that is why you have this book in your hands today.

What I learned in my journey was hard-won, yet simple and effective, and in my time working with female pioneers and leaders, it has become clear to me what makes the elusive difference for successful, high-performing women.

The three stand-out areas which I will introduce in this book are the keys to the kingdom:

- Mastery of focus and effectiveness
- Understanding your personal brand and what makes you unique
- Cultivating a powerful network

There's another magic ingredient that makes a huge difference on what can be a challenging path. **Action. *There is no growth without consistent action.***

I have also included a bonus section in this book on action and accountability, as this is what really makes this work become a part of your daily life. Excellence is, after all, a habit.

Through my work with GameChanger for Women, I have found that the best way to work through this material is as part of a supportive group of women. With this in mind, we

have created just such a group online which you are invited
to join, as my personal guest:

www.gamechanger.vip/community

Focus and Effectiveness - Powering Up Your Productivity

1.

Check In

Let's just check in.

Do you feel that you're always busy, always striving, always doing lots but not quite yielding the results in your business or career that you deserve?

At this juncture, you may need to ask yourself, "Do I truly focus on the things that matter most to me?".

You may find that what matters to you comes further down the list of your priorities than you would ideally like. Family, work, hobbies and more all compete for our mental bandwidth and attention at the same time, often crowding out our ambitions and passions.

You're probably here because you're curious – you want to understand how to boost your impact and how you can do that in the time you have each day, without burnout.

I know how this feels and I can help you find your way through and ensure that you navigate your way to success.

I was an expert juggler and close to burnout at certain points. I was fortunate to realise that something needed to change. My background was in technology, and since then leadership, and I have helped household names and major brands identify strategies, change direction, and engage their people, for over 25 years internationally.

Since then, I've coached leaders in business, entrepreneurs and those looking to take their next step, whether after completing education, spending time raising a family or after big life changes.

The first thing we need to do is to define our clear purpose, essential in creating the necessary focus in striving towards being fully effective.

2.

Understanding Purpose and Applying Focus

What sustains me is understanding my purpose, my key reason for what I do.

My purpose is: **To liberate people's potential**.

This energises and sustains me to access the resources I need to maintain focus and find creative ways through challenges. I can tie back every action I take to linking with this core purpose, which allows me to ensure I give my energy to the right priorities to live this purpose. It's a useful check and guard-rail against distraction or misdirected energy.

I discovered my purpose in 2008 through values elicitation and thinking through my past experiences and current desires. I have added some journal prompts at the end of this section to help you in your reflection towards discovering your purpose.

The reason I share the importance of purpose, in aligning to focus and effectiveness, is specifically for those that came before who were told their success or lack of success was all about time management. This is simply not true – success is about how we apply ourselves, and this bad advice blaming "time" has given rise to many women feeling overwhelmed, burned out and that they had to "do it all".

And so, part of my mission is to correct this for our next generation of women, who deserve to achieve their potential. I dream of a world where women are empowered to be all they can be, and to do this without guilt, fear or shame. I want every woman to reach full potential whilst being able to enjoy life, with good health, relationships, and satisfaction.

Every woman has a unique talent, a unique contribution to make in the world.

I want you to understand for yourself what that purpose, that unique contribution, is for you.

Perhaps you already know this. Perhaps you need some tools to discover it for yourself.

Your core purpose is the impact you want to make on the world around you. Your impact is the change you make, the positive contribution you bring. By the world around you, that can mean locally, within your family, it can be within your community, it can be within your organisation, it can be through your business activities, it can be global. You get to define and choose this for yourself.

The place to start is to define what specifically is the impact that you wish to make. Some people are naturally drawn towards their impact being made through communicating, through teaching; others may find their impact through serving, through caring, through creating.

There are myriad different ways in which we can express our purpose. When we can define our core purpose and allow this to flourish, we impact families, economies, industries, and we can shake the whole world.

Here are some questions you can journal on to reflect on your own impact and purpose, to enable you to apply focus:

Action

My impact: The change I want to make in the world is...

My talents: I will do this by...

Who I serve: The communities I will impact are...

My core purpose statement is that I am here to...

3.

What Applied Focus Can Achieve

So, what can be achieved?

Only you know the truth of that answer for yourself, and I hope you take the leap to find out. What I do know is that the more you can achieve with focus, the more becomes possible, as you integrate your achievements into a strong and positive self-identity and focus on creating further success and strong results.

Some of the highlights that I achieved in my corporate career, once I applied the learning and lessons I share in this book, surpassed my expectations.

Early in my career, by simply focusing on where the strengths were in an organisation that I worked with, spending just two hours on the right thing saved £100,000. This led to my reputation for achieving results beginning to spread.

Spending a couple of days following a process, with a little bit of analysis, on my return from maternity leave, unlocked £300,000 worth of profit in my first week back, leading to me running a profit improvement programme that delivered over £5m on my terms, and being able to use this as a great case study for future projects and to achieve my post-graduate certification.

Then, when I started my own consultancy, just 28 minutes from a first contact with a cold prospect, I secured my first £4,000 client contract as a great start and benchmark to work to. This is something that I now consistently surpass within my business.

Another highlight more recently was spending one day of focused communication with a client last year which identified £25,000 worth of qualified leads. And secured a £250,000 contract for my client.

My clients have also achieved exceptional results – building speaking careers, successful businesses, developing charities and doing work they truly love, building lives they can love too.

Why do I share this? Because these are just small examples of what can be achieved when you give the extra push in the direction of creating focus to your life.

Achieving results, and the change that can be made in all aspects of life, in terms of living standards, happiness, health and relationships was one of the things that excited me about coaching when I took that first step to certification back in 2008.

What has become obvious is that strategies for success which are natural and obvious to the individual are not necessarily natural and obvious to others.

We all have different strengths. That's to be celebrated. When we find something that works, it deserves to be shared, enriching the lives of others.

My hope is that you can take what you need from what I'll share with you here, to apply and implement in your own career, life and business to enrich yourself and those around you.

So, let's dive into some action.

Set yourself up in the best way that works for you – you may choose pen and paper or to use the notepad on your computer. Whatever works, choose a handy way to jot down your reflections, answers and feelings as we take this journey of discovery together. You could even set up a dedicated GameChanger for Women journal to note your reflections as you work through this book.

I'm a great believer in using interactive tools to help to reinforce learnings and embed habits. So, to accompany this book there is a workbook with 21 daily structured exercises to help you along the path towards changing your game. www.gamechanger.vip/community

4.

Start At the Beginning

Right now, I want you to think about what you are truly excellent at.

If there is one thing that you see in yourself or that others see within you, what is it? Where is your excellence?

I'd like you to think about what you love to spend your time doing. It may be in your business or your career, or it may be outside of that, in your personal life or passions. Think of it this way – what would you spend time doing even if you weren't being paid for it? What obsesses you? What results are most important to you?

Different people have different values, desires and wants and different drivers, and that's absolutely okay, we are all individual and unique.

You will know your own benchmark for your own success and setting that should be strictly your own decision.

It may be that you're driven by wealth and that may be wealth in the material sense.

It may be lifestyle and how you choose to live.

It may be time.

It may be your health.

It may be your relationships and the people that you value, those who are close to you or even your day-to-day relationships with the people that you work with.

It may be your growth, and this can be your growth in learning, about acquiring new skills, or it can also be growth in your own personal and philosophical development.

So really think about those things that drive **you**.

Let's be clear, this is not about what other people expect from you, and definitely not what your boss wants you to put here. Let's forget other people for a moment and focus on you.

This is about really getting to the heart of where you excel and your unique DNA, your values and your passions.

Use this information to set your sails, check your compass and get moving in the right direction. It doesn't matter where you are right now, as a small shift in direction will give you different results, so it helps to make sure you are facing the right direction!

Action

Here are some points you can journal on to reflect on your excellence, qualities, values and passions:

I am excellent at...

I love to spend my time...

I'm obsessed with...

I read about...

I would like my results to be...

I'm driven by...

I long for...

Success for me is...

5.

Clarity of Purpose and Choosing In Alignment

Going back to your work in the previous sections, you should now have defined your core purpose in one sentence. The reason I encourage you to do that is so you can refer every decision you make in future about how you allocate your time back to the question: "Does this align with my core purpose?"

I've had many clients that have defined their core purpose as a statement or phrase. They have then had this made into a piece of artwork or a visual aid, visible on their desk or working area, to constantly reinforce the alignment.

Whenever you receive a request which impacts on what you need to choose to do, review it against your core purpose statement. If it fits and is in alignment, it is okay to proceed to get it done. If it doesn't fit, it's not in alignment. If it is not connected with your core purpose or perhaps the happiness of significant people in your life, you must question the value of granting the request, and you need to choose whether to say no.

This technique is something that will begin to get you really focused on what matters for you. It will help you make better and faster decisions as to whether something is a yes or a no.

Your core purpose statement provides a touchstone to refer to, a guide which makes it easier to say no. This is particularly relevant for women – many of us received societal conditioning to "be helpful" and this can make us prone to people-pleasing. This means saying yes, even against our own interests, because we may be worried about negative judgments. For the successful woman, this needs to stop, and the habits of a lifetime may need to change.

If a request doesn't fit with your core purpose, it makes the decision to say "**no**" so much easier.

In allocating our resources of time and energy, it is key to exercise self-compassion and self-discipline.

Be truly honest with yourself about what is achievable within a week.

We only have 24 hours in the day and my recommendation would be that at least 7 to 8 of those should be kept for sleeping.

I know that there are all these tales of people who only need 4 hours' sleep. Trust me, if you are only sleeping for 4 hours a night, you are going to end up exhausted and possibly hit burnout very soon. Adrenal stress, fatigue syndromes and long-term health conditions that can be created because of lack of rest and resourcing are simply not worth it. Your health and wellbeing are key to your long-term success and achieving your mission.

6.

Where Does the Time Go?

Time. If only you had enough of it, right?

We all have the same 24 hours; the only difference is the stuff that we fill those 24 hours with.

We need to look at minimising distractions, even if some of these things can be positive and enjoyable distractions, and there are also often responsibilities we need to pay attention to.

We need to be aware that an intrusion by a distraction, positive or negative, at the wrong time, can pull focus from what's important in any given moment.

One of the biggest challenges, particularly for flexible workers or those running a business, can come from the relationship zone of life. Family and friends. Now, healthy relationships are great. They fill you up, add colour and joy to life and are where you go to for mutual nurturing and support. Unhealthy relationships without boundaries are another matter entirely.

I know about this from my own experience. For most of my career, I was an 'agile worker' which meant that I may be working from the office, I may be working with clients on site, or occasionally I may be working from home. On home-working days, trying to get the family to understand that you are actually working, are not available to run errands and should not be contacted for a chat was one of the big challenges in the early days. Many more have experienced this tussle now, with the increase in hybrid and remote working.

Throw family responsibilities like children or caring for other family members into that mix, and you can be left feeling pulled in all directions at once. It's not a comfortable place to be.

It's something I think that many women, particularly women who are entrepreneurial and trying to build business which they are running, often as a sole trader, can relate too.

What I hear and what is common within the groups that I am part of, is that it can be a real challenge protecting those boundaries.

Let me ask you this.

Does your mission, your purpose, deserve to be nurtured also? Are you worth it?

If so, let's start to look at how you can put practical, loving boundaries in place, which are fair, firm yet flexible.

7.

Value Your Time

We all need to be really honest with ourselves about what can be accomplished within the time we can dedicate to our business or to our career at any given time.

It may be that you're working in a role that is defined as part-time, and it may be that you're contracted to work 5 hours a day for 3 days a week. Don't let this drift into becoming a full-time job by accident. This is something within my corporate career that I saw very frequently. Women had negotiated to work part-time hours, on part-time contracts, because that supported their family.

Typically, in the UK, a part-time contract might look like 3 to 4 days a week where the woman is expected to work from 9.30 am to 3.00 pm on each of those days. The reality was that quite often, when I reviewed with these colleagues what they were actually undertaking and the job function that they were performing, they were being expected to deliver the same results as somebody being paid a full-time salary on a full-time contract.

Additionally, we find in studies that part-time employees are actually working the same effective hours as a full-timer, if not more, to deliver their results – because the full-time office employee can be only 70% (and maybe less!) productive, spending the other 30% of their time on office gossip and water-cooler breaks, and being paid for that inefficient time.

This bind of part-time working women to overdeliver but yet take a pay sacrifice can occur because they do not feel confident and empowered to push back and challenge what is realistic and achievable within those part-time hours.

Now, I don't know about you, but I really do not think working full-time hours for part-time pay is a definition of success. Analyse your diary and look at what was achieved against your planned time. Did you underestimate the time that a given task would take? Did you build in time to deal with the unexpected and reactive work? Plan in your time for reactive work, as well as your planned activities to drive forward.

8.

Perfectionism and Procrastination - 2 Sides of the Same Coin

Evaluate your working standards. I find a common issue with high-achieving female clients around perfectionism and procrastination.

Many people that I have coached suffer with the perfectionism/procrastination bind. They will often craft and review to create something that's 100% perfect, and in doing so, deliver it late or in a desperate rush. Often this is giving more than needs to be given. 80% and on time might be a more appropriate priority. If you feel resistance to this statement, this may be an area you need to pay attention to.

This is not a case for lowering standards. Quite often, the deadline and flow of work or release of ideas to collaborate is what is important. You can still do work to a great quality but that extra 20% finessing a proposal could possibly have been better spent elsewhere. That final 20% is not going to yield 80% of the results. It's probably going to be the first 20% of the work you put into a task that is going to yield 80% of the results, if you're planning and preparing effectively.

9.

Nailing Email

L et's start with an easy one. E-mail. E-mail can be a huge source of distraction.

Research by Baydin in 2012 showed that the average user received 147 e-mails per day. That's just an average. And that's before the explosion of email marketing and social media adding massively to the time distractions online.

I know that towards the tail end of my corporate career in 2014, I was receiving close to 500 business e-mails a day, let alone any personal ones.

So, what do we need to do to handle this deluge of material?

Use auto-responders to structure senders' expectations as to when you will respond to emails. Not every email should be expecting an immediate response! Set up redirects to more appropriate people for certain enquiries. Actively and ruthlessly unsubscribe to emails which serve no purpose! Set up sub-folders for categories of email, to avoid a massive single inbox. By getting organised, you can get your checking and responses to emails down to less than 30 minutes a day.

With any email, one of three things needs to happen:

Act - you may need to act on an email, by calling, replying or delegating.

File - you may simply need to retain the information for future use.

Delete - you may have no use at all for the email and its information, so let it go.

Educate people about your email preferences. Have set times to respond and set a clear expectation of your response timescales. And don't send unnecessary emails yourself when a phone call is more effective and immediate!

10.

'Not-So-Social' Social Media

The next often maligned time thief is social media – if you allow it to be!

Most women that I'm connected with professionally use social media and it is a powerful tool when used well.

However, a lot of people talk about 'falling into the Facebook vortex' or 'doomscrolling', where people can just end up spending time scrolling through social media to pass the time with no useful purpose in mind.

It's common now to see people and families going out for dinner. With their phones on the table.

Should we give our time and presence to a mobile phone? Or is it best giving presence and attention to the people that we are with, that have chosen to spend time with us.

Turn the phone and socials off from time to time, set limits and minimise notifications where you can, and have set times each week to respond and deal only with what's important.

If you use social media to build relationships, use it strategically and with a clear purpose in mind that you can measure against.

Be aware you are the commodity, your data is valuable, and that social media is designed to change your neurological responses, to get you to spend more time online, giving more of your precious data to advertisers.

You need to control it, so that it doesn't control you.

11.

Information Overload

_____

We are bombarded from all sides – by the internet, TV and other media... so, are you consuming information for information's sake?

We can all learn, but being selective over what we consume, whether that's books, audio books, podcasts, videos, seminars, training, is the key.

Be highly selective and make sure what you choose to consume is directed towards where you want your area of excellence to be.

Know why you are reading, watching or listening to something.

Understand where you are going to create most value from the right information, that is key. You need to understand what output or creativity is going to come from your input of consuming more information.

Good stuff in = good stuff out. Raise the quality.

12.

The Other Stuff

Poor health is another area in life where distraction, in this case through pain, can sap your focus and energy.

The paradox is that pursuing a healthy lifestyle can quite often be neglected because you are time poor due to the other distractions creeping in elsewhere. An example is not dealing with health problems as soon as they arise, with either a correction in behaviour or diet or a visit to a health professional.

Make time for eating healthily and exercising well, by planning ahead and creating routine.

Other distractions and time thieves that can slow you down are worry, stress, the state of your finances, your boss or any number of people you interact with on a daily basis. It can be your environment, or it could be your colleagues.

Think about each of these areas in turn.

Think about what makes you feel energised and what saps your soul, causing distraction and drains on your time.

A plan to maximise your time

Make 2 lists – what you want more of, the productive stuff which feeds into your purpose, and what you want to avoid, the distractions which pull you away from this. Start shifting the dial.

I want more...	I want less...

13.

Saying "No" and Holding Boundaries

Saying "No" can be tough and may mean you need to have some conversations which may not be easy, where you share your new ground rules and make it clear that you are making some changes in your life.

You can do this elegantly and with grace and you do not need to offer explanations, unless you want to, when you feel the person will support you in your changes.

As individuals, we can put immense pressure on ourselves by not using the power of an effective "No", so think realistically about what is possible for you and where your limits are.

This is not saying you can't achieve anything you want to set out to achieve, or to place limitations. Understand that achievement also requires that you are going to need to say no with discernment to requests and bids for time that are not adding value to what you want in your career, business or life.

Healthy ways to say "No" to requests that don't honour your time and your goals need to be honest and empowered responses.

You can say "No" and guide people to a more appropriate person to help them.

You can say "No, not right now" to put something off until it is more reasonable/suitable for you to devote time to.

In the right circumstances, you can simply say "No", and thank the other person for thinking of you.

You do not owe excuses to anybody.

14.

Your Environment

One of the best ways to minimise distraction and increase inspiration is by de-cluttering our environment.

Think about the layout of your home and workspaces and make sure that things are within easy reach for the task that you want to perform.

Have organised and simple filing systems so that you know where you are going to find things, whether it's digital files, or physical books, journals and papers.

Use design and think about where you move objects from and to. Think about for what purpose, where and how items are stored. Keep lines simple and allow clear flow in your space.

The old adage of 'a place for everything and everything in its place' works, both for the physical and for information.

Look at automating tasks where possible if there are repetitive tasks requiring little attention.

Use time blocking and group activities and tasks together in batches.

15.

More Time For What You Love...

Do you often find yourself over-committed?

Beyond the setting of boundaries to banish over-commitment, now we've looked at ways to minimise small distractions, the best way to find more time for what you love is to examine your daily habits.

Where can you make productive changes?

Are you beginning to get a clear picture of what you want more of?

Nature fills gaps, so scheduling and carving out time for the things that you do want in your life is important. I'm really old-school with this and therefore recommend a page-a-day diary as well as your online scheduler.

A great place to start is to make sure that you have time for movement and exercise or gym visits scheduled in your diary, so that you can sustain working at optimum health.

This helps you to be more effective during your focused periods of working, whether on business, your passions or a creative project. By ensuring that you take care of your health, the area that is often the first to get neglected when we have many commitments, you are setting yourself up for success by laying the right and strong foundations.

So, this task just requires a little of self-honesty and self-reflection here. One of the things that I quite often take my clients through is to have a long, hard look at what's going on in their diary and in their life.

I am an absolute Outlook fan. I use it for scheduling everything and if it's not in my Outlook, it does not happen. This is great as it provides a clear record of time spent and how, and you can easily review past months and years.

Whether you use a notebook or a calendar – look at the balance in your life. I use colour-coding to identify different "zones" such as wellness, working on goals, family time, study, social time and other areas of my life which are important to me.

Look at each of the days of the week and notice how many hours you are spending on rest and relaxation as well as your other commitments.

I am going to be radical and request that we prioritise rest and relaxation first. Without it, there is no foundation for health and wellbeing.

I understand that this is a challenge. I have had times in my life when the amount of work was too much. I was studying at post-graduate level at the same time as holding down a demanding corporate career, so I had the balance wrong and the end result was stress. Luckily, I was able to course correct quickly and started to prioritise breathwork, yoga and meditation.

You can end up overwrought, burnt out, working crazy hours and not knowing which way is up when you don't prioritise or even know how to relax.

The two most important things that you need to schedule are your rest and your relaxation. Make sure you put the big rocks in your jar first.

If you have a sleep requirement for 7 hours a night, 8 hours a night, 9 hours a night, whatever it is, that is individual and personal to you, so **you** need to make sure that you fill that cup first.

16.

Do, Delegate or Ditch

The next area for scrutiny is to look at what time you spend within your household, on the things that need to be done there, like routine tasks and maintenance. I would also ask the question, could there be a better balance for those of you that live with family or significant others? Would it be more beneficial to hire a gardener or cleaner, and what value would that give in terms of time back with your loved ones?

Look at the time that you spend creating the right environment for yourself.

Look at the things that are team tasks, then look at your productive tasks and also ensure you schedule time in for creative and strategic thinking.

So, for each of these areas, look at this and see what you are actually doing within the week – that's just a week of doing a little bit of time recording, a little bit of focus on where your time is going.

You could use Outlook or a physical diary and pen and paper. You could use a time-measuring app. Searching for 'task time tracker' in app stores reveals several great free tools you can use.

Whatever you choose, use something that is going to make it easy for you to record a variety of activities, however mundane, and try and be conscious and mindful of where you are spending your time. Track your actions and activities versus where you think you would like to be spending your time, and then reflect on what your ideal balance would look like.

The questions to ask yourself in each of these areas should focus on your enjoyment, your productivity and the output from each task or activity you choose to invest your time in. Here are some examples of questions you might reflect on:

Did I enjoy this activity?

Has this activity advanced my core purpose and my mission?

How did I feel when completing this activity?

Did the activity energise me or drain me?

What is the actual or expected outcome from the activity?

Look at how your energy levels are affected, and whether the activity aligns with your strengths and talents. This can help you to determine whether you should spend either more or less time on these activities. You may choose to delegate some of these activities to a virtual assistant if they are not aligned to your talents or are time intensive and low return. With some domestic chores, if applicable, have an honest discussion with your family about what represents a fair distribution of tasks.

Ask yourself what value these activities are bringing to your life.

Then, consider what is a realistic future balance and solution. For example, I freely admit I do not love housework or cleaning. Some people do. So, for me, it is a sound investment for me to hire people who will do this for me, to give me more time to work on the strategy of my business and stay energised.

Think about your own typical weekly flow and define what is ideal for you. Think about each activity and how you would rate your current performance or level of satisfaction in each of these areas. Then simply decide whether to continue to do it, delegate or ditch entirely.

Sample list:

Do	Delegate	Ditch
Business development	Delivery	WhatsApp
School pickup	Cleaning	News
Personal finance	Business accounts	In-person shopping

17.

Dance to Your Own Rhythm

Another key aspect to being successful in maintaining focus and effectiveness is to understand your energy levels and natural body clock, your circadian rhythm. There's some great data visualisation on this that has been done by Info We Trust (https://infowetrust.com/project/routines) which visualised and created infographics of some of the daily routines of the world's greatest influencers and thinkers from many creative disciplines and sciences. This illustrates the variability of schedules and the many ways we can energise ourselves to achieve our core purpose and mission. There is no such thing as typical. This was based on source data from the book, *Daily Rituals: How Artists Work* by Mason Currey.

The key for you is to experiment and get to know your right pace and flow. In my corporate career, as an early agile worker, with the ability to choose to work from home, I realised I favoured early morning working for my deep, focused work. For meetings and collaboration, the sweet spot was from 10am. My preference was then to spend time outdoors or exercising, for at least an hour between 12-2, with problem solving and more deep work into the afternoon and early evening.

Lifestyle changes altered this, as did becoming the director of my own company.

Now, I love an early start at 5am, as this works for my clients in the Middle East too.

If I'm with a client in the working day, I'll break and have family time, with good music and conversation over breakfast between 7.30 and 8.45. This shifts my energy and gives me a boost with connection and affection before a day in the office.

I'll hold client meetings and calls between 10-2, then make time usually to do the school run at 3pm, with then family time until 6pm.

If it's not a client day, after the school run, I'll hit the gym, work out, and then work on projects instead between 10-2.

The evenings are my time for me to read, research and work on business development and strategy in a relaxed pace, or to hire a babysitter and enjoy some social time or business networking events, again, as connection is important to me and fills my cup.

Weekends are committed to fun with the family, with a little enjoyable business reading, planning and research in the early morning and late evening, if I feel called to do so.

I also worked out, during the pandemic, that I'm a big fan of early bedtimes before 10pm!

So, knowing what energises you and building in time for this, like the connection time, family and gym or spa, for me is as important as designated productive time. When I relax,

I have my best strategic leaps forward, by being in the mode of relaxed performance.

If you want to generate great ideas, take a walk or a holiday, and see what happens. When the mind is lucid, it connects ideas more readily and creatively.

Understand what helps **you** achieve focus. For me, if I'm doing deep work or a project, I need a quiet environment with electronic background music. I need a clear area and surfaces and I need pen and paper to doodle ideas that come to me in the process.

Understand yourself and what makes you happiest in your working environment.

I balance my week best by having 20 hours of direct client contact a week, as I am an ambivert – but that means in my time away from clients, I need to minimise any external contact and distractions, as I need time by myself to be creative.

Understand your likes, needs, desires and values to create structures that work for you. Ensure you energise and relax in equal measure to build resilience and protect yourself from burnout. Your core purpose and your mission and talents are too important to allow that to happen!

Another beauty of rituals, structure, routine and ordered flow, is that in creating this, we can plan time for the spontaneous and unstructured things in life, allowing us greater freedom and enjoyment in our leisure time. I get a huge amount done, but I take leisure time every day.

18.

Embrace Pleasure

In the early 2000s I was introduced to the concept of the holi-hour – not a holiday – but just an hour dedicated to enjoyment and pleasure each day. To see pleasure as a daily requirement, key to my performance and wellbeing was truly a #GameChanger!

I also followed advice to try something new each day – whether a new walking route, listening to a new album, going to an exhibition. The importance of this daily habit is to stimulate the human need for novel and new experience.

There's another advantage to taking heed of this advice – new experiences can lead us to discover new passions, and also to build new neural pathways. This can protect our cognitive health. It also makes us more cultured and enriched individuals and can help with problem-solving by promoting flexibility in thinking and responses.

19.

Seek Simplicity

In daily decision-making, we can use up energy, known as decision fatigue. It's an often-quoted fact that Steve Jobs and Mark Zuckerburg were both fans of wearing the same type of clothing every day.

Now, as a woman, I enjoy expressing myself through fashion and I'm not suggesting we go quite as far as that. I like to have a bit of variety in my wardrobe, but I do have a go-to signature style, which makes my packing for international trips simpler, faster and easier. The bonus is that it keeps my appearance on brand.

What we are aiming for is simplicity in routine. So, if your thing is wild shoes, go for it, and change them up with a uniform look in your clothing. Make that your distinction.

I also highly recommend a wardrobe edit and career/ business 'uniform' to make the most of the right purchases and to develop a signature style. More on that in the Personal Branding section!

20.

Choosing the Right Routine - Pick & Mix!

We all have different rhythms. The better that you can understand your own rhythms, the more you will be able to choose to do tasks at a time that is optimum for you. There is no one daily routine that works for everybody, nor does one routine fit all of the time and this is why most attempts at structure fail.

It may not be the same routine every day. For me, it is certainly not the same every day because I must balance my business with being a lone parent to three children, while still undertaking international travel for client assignments and business networking. All this while still maintaining a social life and a decent level of health.

I have 5 daily routines:

1. Family Day
2. Personal Day (Restorative)
3. Client Day (UK)
4. Client Day (International)
5. Internal Project Day (UK)

Each may be in different time zones, but the daily structure for each type of day is a given.

I review each type of daily structure periodically to make sure it's matching my current health and energy needs, as, particularly as women, we need to account for the hormonal fluctuations that can influence our energy and wellbeing from time to time.

In the seasonal cycle, I have more rest periods in the summer to enjoy the season and strategise, and my intense delivery period with clients is usually from August to the end of the year.

January and February are a strategic time for growth, with another intense period from March to June. Knowing this seasonal variation, I can adapt my routines to maximise the changing daylight hours, and client demand.

21.

Set Motivating Goals

---

key part of focus is the diligence to **do what you must**.

This is really where we look at our concrete plans and taking action, so go back to your earlier observations to reflect on your talents and skills.

Think about your top five personal goals* for success, for the next three months. Note them down in your journal.

How will you measure yourself and define if your next three months have been successful and created positive change for you?

*Please resist the temptation to add six/seven goals, that's not the objective here. Limit yourself to five because if you're going beyond this, you start needing to ask which are more important. So, there are only five slots to fill here, as this is an exercise in prioritising and decision-making.

Limiting this to five will reinforce the learning around boundaries and being realistic about what's possible.

When defining your top five, clearly identify why each goal is something that is important and meaningful to you.

Define your top five goals

Use the box below to write down an initial version of your top five goals.

It is important to explore what the feelings and emotional connections are around each of your five goals. Emotion is what moves us to action.

Now create a map or plan as to how you will achieve each of these goals. What is the logical next step? What resources do you need? Enjoy getting into the thinking about what will support you to achieve your goals.

22.

Accept Support

Superwoman is not real!

One of my first coaching clients, back in 2008, was a lady who was managing one of those part-time careers which was actually full-time hours. The client had a young family and a husband who was in a completely different career and didn't really understand her job.

One of the issues my client experienced was negotiating support – agreeing what he could do and what support and commitments he would make with childcare, household chores and social arrangements. The client had a very traditional domestic set-up – in the past all the expectation for these challenges had fallen on the woman in the relationship.

We worked together through a timetabling exercise and looked at where she was being asked to achieve the impossible. There simply wasn't the time to do it all. My client needed to negotiate that support. With her partner, my client created time to have a conversation around their commitments and the needs of the family. What helped her in negotiating was having a clear vision and structured, meaningful goals. Her husband came to understand that through supporting her and sharing responsibilities, he could also help her to further her career. As well as a positive financial impact on the family which meant better possibilities for their future and for their children, he understood that this made a massive contribution to his wife's levels of happiness and satisfaction.

By going through that process of identifying the emotional connection to goals, you can create a more powerful framework for negotiating with the people who you need to support you. This skill is crucial.

A support network is incredibly valuable, and you must nurture this. Post-divorce and as a lone parent, one of the things that has really enabled me to successfully run my business has been being able to reach out to a trusted network of friends. I can ask for support, such as with childcare if I've got a meeting with a client or even overseas travel. A big step for me was realising that I do need people to step in, to support and help out, and to take on various roles for me rather than me trying to manage singlehandedly.

23.

Commit to Yourself

Visualise the steps to your success.

Be specific on how you plan to achieve success towards each of your five goals.

Think about when the best time is to take action. Many people have writing as a goal and will reserve time in the early hours of the morning or in those late hours of the evening to take focused time to write or to create content.

Whether it's working on a business plan because you are looking at transitioning out of a corporate career, or learning a new skill, you must have a plan. Make working on your plan a ritual that you do each day or on specific days of the week, as this will move you towards your goal.

With successful, creative people, it is also **how** they work which is important.

Maya Angelou's daily routine was worked out in detail. She found that the best place for her to conduct her writing was in hotels. It was an environment where she could isolate herself and be uninterrupted in order to access her creative flow.

Some people work best in long stretches, others prefer short sprints. You will know what you prefer for different types of tasks.

You will know when your best time is to be making phone calls and undertaking external and sociable tasks rather than conducting focused research alone.

For certain tasks, I purposely disconnect the internet and set the phone to 'Do not disturb' because I know I need to stay totally focused, particularly for financial and strategic planning.

What do you need to have around you as you begin?

It may be having the right technology, the right supplies of stationery, the tools for the task at hand. Think about every aspect of the set-up to work at your most effective before you begin in any endeavour.

Understand what causes resistance and what the payoffs may be.

When you're not achieving what you want to achieve, reflect and explore what's causing that.

It may simply be waiting for the perfect time.

It may be resistance to working under pressure, if you are a 'rebel' archetype. I call this the 'freedom illusion', which is the belief that "I'll do it when I feel like it". This often has roots in subconscious rebellion, from over-control by others in the past. This needs to be worked on, ideally with a coach or therapist, if this is sabotaging your achievements.

If there is some subconscious rebelling going on, possibly because you have felt highly constrained by previous working environments, I can assure you that even within a corporate structure, you do not have to work in a 9 to 5 way.

You need to look at what works productively for you, and negotiate the boundaries, negotiate how that works with your team.

You will find that if you are working to your own rhythm, your productivity improves and to be fair, that's the name of the game in business.

Does any of this resonate with you – are you in resistance?

Once you can recognise this, you can take action to deal with it professionally and consciously to stop the resistance and inner rebel from sabotaging your success.

24.

Breaking Through Overwhelm

If you are feeling overwhelmed with a task and struggling to complete it, or even to make a start on it, a helpful technique is to reflect on when you completed something successfully which has similar traits to the task in hand.

Think back to that scenario – how did you feel and what worked?

An example is report writing. Most people need to write reports in some way, shape or form in their career. How did you feel and what worked when you produced a really great quality report?

Ask yourself the question, "How will I, at my best, approach this task?"

This will unlock creativity and move you into a sense of flow as you imagine your approach and how you will take action.

I always think it's helpful to make this stage of planning and breaking through as enjoyable as possible. That can be by adding music, it can be your environment, it can be funky stationery, it can be whatever works for you.

You may say, I work in an office, it's not possible for me to listen to music in the office. Take a pair of headphones.

I did this in corporate. I would go into the office early before everybody else, and I would begin my day with headphones on, listening to what I wanted to listen to, before the phones were ringing.

This was great, as this meant I wasn't playing catch-up. My emails were cleared, my day mapped out, I knew what I needed to do, anything urgent was dealt with.

The simple thing of having half an hour of music to start my day got me through my tasks much more quickly than without.

Some people like to work in silence, some people prefer background noise, we are each unique in this respect.

If you are still struggling to make a start, use the timer on your phone to commit to setting aside 20 minutes for planning the activity or project.

That 20 minutes might simply be used to break down and plan how you're going to tackle the task, thinking about what support and resources you might need. Whatever it is, just make a start with 20 minutes. It will fly by, and you will probably find that you do now want to carry on and continue, if you are in your flow.

If not, you've at least got the rudiments of a plan and you can go back to the task at a suitable point now that you've broken it down into manageable parts.

25.

Mindfulness Breaks

Think about your top three tasks in each day. Note these on a card, Post-it note or in your diary.

I recommend one task is something urgent, another is strategic and an investment to your long-term success, and the final task is focused on your learning or wellbeing.

Then, build in mindfulness breaks within your day. At three points in the day, set a reminder to pause and breathe. Then, reflect on your progress on your three tasks before picking back up with your work.

This was something I adopted after I had my first daughter when I returned to corporate, when she was six months old. The pause, cultivating a presence in the moment, developed an ability in me to come back to centre, back from those points where there were many demands externally, and come back to clarity and full focus.

I would set myself three mindfulness bells in the day.

I would take one break at 10am, which is often the point when a working day may be starting to get derailed, particularly if you are in a client facing role, where firefighting and problem solving are key.

The next mindfulness bell was at 1pm, which signalled the afternoon slot when the phone starts ringing and everybody's emails have been sent over the lunchtime period.

Finally, the last mindfulness bell I would take note of would be at 3pm and for that one I would just create a minute of silence and then simply review the top three tasks list that I had created in the morning.

Had all the tasks been ticked off? If not, reviewing at 3pm meant that there were a couple of hours within the normal working day to put in place any strategies that were needed to recover and achieve what was needed.

26.

The Importance of Reward and Celebration

Look for opportunities to build in small rewards throughout the day to sustain motivation and keep your energy high.

I used to reward myself for submitting my expenses. I dislike repetitive tasks and recording and claiming expenses was one task that I would often leave. It would be something I would do once a month rather than throughout the week on an ongoing basis. For repetitive tasks, I prefer to batch them and do them all at once.

My reward to myself for successful completion was booking tickets to the ballet or theatre. Every time I completed the month's submission, I could reward myself by booking tickets to go and see something that I really wanted to go and see, using some of the money being repaid back to me as a result of completing my expenses!

However, reward often becomes intrinsic once you've completed a task. It's the satisfaction of a task well done.

You may need little motivators to get you going and they can be as big or as small as you choose. However, when you've completed something, allow yourself that moment or two of quiet reflection afterwards to celebrate a job well done.

27.

Final Words on Focus

The key lessons on focus and effectiveness that really contribute to your personal excellence are:

1. **Make rest and relaxation a priority.**

2. **Work to your energy levels.** As you take on each task, understand whether it's something that nourishes you or whether it's something that drains you. We want more of the good stuff and less of the bad stuff.

3. **Review and reflect.** This is so important so please don't drop your review and reflection time out of your day. It's not something that's optional. Review and reflection allow us to be in this process of continual refinement so that we can produce our best work.

4. **Set clear goals.** Clarity and purpose in your chosen direction is essential.

5. **Be organised.** This saves so much time! Make sure you have the right equipment, resources, people and structures that you need to help you perform at your best.

6. **Create the right environment.** An environment which inspires you, one which helps you to produce your best work, whatever that may be. It may be that you need some variety as well, so perhaps choose different working environments for different types of tasks.

7. **Exercise self-compassion and self-discipline.** We are all human. Being able to exercise self-compassion and self-discipline is being able to honour the self. If we honour ourselves, and the purpose we have committed to, and have the self-esteem to be able to do that effectively, this creates strong self-efficacy. It promotes a virtuous circle where others see that we have that level of self-belief and self-respect. This supports us in our confidence and self-esteem, which improves how we project ourselves and how we relate to others.

SECTION 2:

Personal Brand

28.

What is Your Personal Brand?

Your personal brand is how you communicate with people your authentic values, strengths and stance in this world. It is how you put your stamp on your life roles and achievements, whether you are in an organisation or running your own business.

It's much more than headshots, a logo and a colour scheme.

- It's sharing with people the value that you bring to any interaction, to any piece of work that you are doing with them.
- It's looking at your authenticity and what is completely unique about you.
- Some people would define it as who you are.
- It's about your unique point of value.

Think about what you bring, whether it's to a project or to a team, or to a committee that you may sit on, or any other relevant roles where you show up and contribute.

What do you bring that is different? What do you bring that nobody else can?

It may be that you're the person that brings the social fun. You may be the person who brings the eye for detail. We all have many, many different qualities that we bring to our interactions with others.

We'll do some reflection in this section.

Hopefully you've got a pen and paper to hand so that you can make some notes as we go through, to look back on your reflections from earlier sections and reflect on what we cover moving forward. We'll cover why personal brand is important and how you define this. You will be able to articulate what you want to be known for.

We'll examine how you communicate your personal brand and look at how you can consistently put that into practice.

29.

Your Unique Value

What is the unique value that you bring to your interactions, to your business, to your career?

Let's think about why this is important.

Firstly, pick any brand or public figure who represents a personal brand to you.

An example I use when teaching this is the late Dame Vivienne Westwood.

Probably when you think of UK icons, Vivienne Westwood was probably somebody that represented the 'Best of British' on an international stage, with brand recognition and influence on fashion globally, at the forefront of the UK fashion industry for close to 50 years.

There were some highly distinctive things about Dame Vivienne's personal brand.

She was known for being a little bit risqué, a little bit edgy. Synonymous with the punk movement in art, music and fashion. If you said to somebody Vivienne Westwood, they would have an idea immediately and visually of what her personal brand was about, through the distinctive style and reference points, and the interviews with her and profiles over the years.

Our personal brand is the expression of that unique value that we bring, and it is communicated through signs and signals. These may be visual, verbal or non-verbal – it's the tone of our website, it's how we curate our social media, the opinions and interests we share, and how we show to others who we are.

Partly, it could be your logo if you're in business. It could be from the way you style yourself through your clothes and appearance in your career, and in your personal life.

Many of us have signature traits, quirks and styles, and our friends usually know us well enough to look at something, even whether it's a pair of shoes in a store to say, "That's so you".

So, think about your personal brand. Is it elegance? Is it simplicity? Is it ultra-feminine? There are so many different qualities that you may choose to focus on to begin to develop your personal brand.

Take time to find out what makes you unique, what makes you valuable and how you bring this into your personal brand. Your brand is as much about what you understand yourself to be as how you choose to communicate this to others.

What this enables, if you are in business, is for your prospective and existing customers to identify, buy from and work with the real and authentic you, with you represented to your best.

And if you are building your profile for your career, it makes you memorable to those you meet, and also signals if you are somebody your peers, clients and colleagues can promote and build success with.

There's an old sales saying, that 'People like people like them'. However, in my experience, this is over-simplistic and doesn't fully reflect our experience. While we might gravitate towards people who are similar to us, in a sales context, the people we may be attracted to are those who we admire, have charisma and stand out from the crowd, even if this is done in a subtle way.

30.

The Real You

Take a pen and paper and identify your five favourite words to describe yourself.

As with the exercise earlier, just limit yourself to five.

If you think of more, just put them down in a column on one side of your paper, as these may be aspects of your character you may want to come back to.

For now, decide on the five words which are the most representative.

And then I'd like you to think about how your best friend or how a member of your family might describe you to other people.

Do the descriptions line up? Are you the same on the inside, and how you see yourself, as how others see you, or is there a gap to address and close?

The characteristics of our personal brand are what become the outward facing version of you, and so they are even more about how others see us as opposed to how we see ourselves.

To live and work with honesty and integrity though, these two perspectives need to be congruent with each other.

If you think that you come across as highly organised and efficient, but people actually see you as bubbly, vivacious and fun, and not particularly organised, then there's a huge difference in your brand message and you need to understand what that difference is.

Your brand is an extension of you, so it helps to understand and work with your personal definition and play to your strengths. It is how you express what is uniquely and authentically you – naturally and without forcing it – so that this is consistent every time. This builds trust and a tribe and shows your unique value promise to people.

Reflect on your core purpose statement from the previous chapters, and what matters to you most.

What are the most important things to you in your business or career? Here is a list of some key potential factors – which ones would you tick and want to see reflected in your personal brand?

- Innovation and creativity
- Passion and connecting
- Power
- Prestige
- Trust and loyalty
- An air of mystique
- Alertness and an attention to detail

So, why do you need to be clear and focused on which of these are important to you in your business or career?

Whatever your business or vocation is, you need to be making it personal.

Your connections are with people and the best relationships are built on trust and connection. And that can only be achieved by being your authentic self... the real you.

31.

Building Trust

People hire or people buy from people who they know, like and trust. That makes it really important that it's the real you that your customers or clients or colleagues connect with.

I have found this to be extremely important, which is why I am sharing this.

In my corporate career, I worked mainly with major brands. In managing client relationships, it was as much about the client buying into me personally as it was about them buying into the brand that I was representing. It was important for me when I was performing that role to be in alignment with the brand that I was working for, whilst still expressing my unique value for innovation, creativity and finding solutions – which is where **GameChanger** started, as this was a word a client used to describe what I brought to the table.

Every role in every business has a customer impact which either expresses or contradicts brand values. Imagine that you work for a bank. Recently, I had a fantastic experience with my bank. I went in person to my bank branch to take care of some business, and what was great was that I walked away from the interaction thinking how pleased I was with this bank. I've used that bank for 30 years now and the interaction was not particularly complicated or unusual. I won't mention which bank it is, but what was unique about the interaction was the person representing the brand.

Unusually, this bank is trying to put forward a much more approachable face with its customers and that really came through in the warmth of the person serving me, delivering the best service to me. So it was as much about the person representing the brand having the right values, and demonstrating their trustworthiness, as it was about the prestige brand and the big logo.

This is where brands build loyalty – in evoking emotion, feeling, warmth and resonance.

One of the quotes that I often share is from Winston Churchill, that "All the great things are simple", and that's why when I've asked you to think about your own brand, I am asking you to distil that to the essence of just five words. Five words that can work for you.

As you grow teams and businesses, those five words will become a touchstone, so your personal brand is reflected in the quality and leadership of all that you do.

32.

The Impact of Personal Brand Values

I spoke with a client recently who had gone through the exercise with me a few months before at a live workshop of defining her personal brand.

This client manages a team of several people, it's her business, and she has a number of associates working with her.

Her personal brand now carries through into her company brand and that has allowed her to create a value statement which she has given to her associates.

Interestingly, what she shared with me recently is that this has also enabled her to evaluate the opportunities that are coming to her through the lens of whether they align with her personal brand. This may be new clients, or new opportunities to market and collaborate.

This is making it much easier for her to say yes to the right things, and no to those that do not align, to ensure that she keeps the right focus.

Building on the core purpose work we undertook earlier in the book, what value do you add to everything that you do? Here are a couple of examples:

- Making sure that things are as perfect as they can be before they are released.
- Making sure that people are taken care of, with warmth and hospitality.

It may help to ask other people this question about you. What value do your colleagues believe you add?

Our strengths and the value we bring can be very, very different things.

The impact on your business and career of a strong personal brand is to allow you to be memorable and recognised. It builds affinity. It allows you to be congruent, so you are saving time in your messaging, as the words and offers you make come from the heart, not the head.

When you're creating a strong personal brand from a place of congruence, you instinctively know how you are going to approach something. You know how to communicate effectively, and you know how this is going to be received by your stakeholders.

It makes life and business so much easier.

I've written many articles and had many speaking engagements in the corporate world and in leadership seminars, where the key message is on the importance of being yourself and showing up as yourself.

What you must remember, even if you are working in a relatively large organisation, perhaps one where you feel there is a strong corporate identity and uniformity, is that they hired you to **be you**.

You were already enough, and you were what they were looking for. Many people forget this crucial aspect.

Your organisation hired you for your unique contribution, for your ideas, for your ability to connect with people. They didn't hire somebody else. Your organisation wants you to be you and use your unique talents and strengths to win and grow business.

If people know what you can do, they will also think of you first.

33.

The Link Between Authenticity and Performance

Being yourself and creating a strong personal brand which enables you to show up fully as yourself is important. When we are in alignment and congruent with our values, beliefs and desires, we are operating from true authenticity, and this reflects in our performance.

When we are not being ourselves, and instead act as we think others expect, to achieve a goal or outcome, that stifles us – we are goal-attached, not service-focused, so the intention and energy are different. Crucially, that can be felt by our colleagues or clients and can move us further away from what we desire.

This is quite common with graduates or early career stage candidates in large organisations, as they may need to develop the inner confidence to stand for who they are.

When we are operating from a false self, our communication is not clear. Additionally, there are often defence mechanisms that come into play that can block our natural rapport building.

The false self being projected, as a false self-construct, is because we fear who we might be and how that authentic self might be rejected by others. And so, our ego protects us by putting on a mask.

This is something very powerful to work with, to make big transformations moving forward.

A great question to ask yourself is whether you can acknowledge and list all the things that are great about you.

Like most people I coach, you may (and probably will) feel a resistance.

"That's bragging."
"I should be humble."
"What if I come across as arrogant?"
"What if they think I am bossy or know too much?"
"What if they don't like me?"
"What if they don't accept me?"

Now, all of this is natural and normal – we are, after all, social creatures.

However, look at that shadow creeping up. Examine it deeply.

What's your fear of what you might be?
Who might you be if you did actually know it all?
Who might you be if you were powerful?
Who might you be if you had unshakeable confidence?
Who would you be if you walked in as if you owned the room and had a right to be there?

***

What would concern you if other people were saying it about you outside of the room to others?

The reason I ask is because this can also help us in understanding our authentic selves. Over time, your authentic self changes, through life stages, learning and new experiences, so never accept that this is static. I tend to review and check in with myself quite regularly, at least yearly. Over time we develop and are drawn to different archetypes. Understanding who we fear we might be and how that might be causing us to project a false sense of self is intense and deep internal work. It is important to undertake this exercise, to uncover your true self beneath the beliefs, constructs and norms you have grown with to date.

Peace and ease come from being true to yourself, which makes expressing your personal brand so much simpler.

34.

The Authentic Self

In the companion workbook, available at www.gamechanger.vip/community there are helpful exercises to discover your authentic self in more depth.

We become congruent and self-aware when we have taken the time to explore our thoughts and beliefs about who we are in the world, and we come to accept the parts of us that we were worried were unacceptable or unlovable to others. This process is not a one-off exercise – it's a life's work of discovery, enquiry and refinement as we reach for our true potential. The paradox is that the conclusion we should eventually reach is an acceptance that we are enough already.

People use the phrase 'comfortable in our own skin'. We all see and recognise those who are truly comfortable in their own skin and accepting of their specific physicality. They have a presence and a calmness that is palpable.

When we can say we are truly comfortable in our skin, that we can dance to the beat of our own drum, we are able to show our authentic self without fear of judgement from others.

The magic of this is that the authentic self is the one that attracts and resonates most with other people. It is our true nature, our innocence, our 'golden child' archetype, for whom everything is playful, light and enjoyable. That feeling is the one where you are being your authentic self.

Take a moment to think back to the last time you felt that joy, ease, grace and lightness.

Was it last week?
Last month?
Last year?
Last decade?
In your childhood?

It really does not matter when it was, on your timeline. What matters is that you can recall and tap into that feeling and that essence. Remember who you are in your wholeness, before people began labelling, judging, or telling you who you were. You have power.

In our full and authentic expression of ourselves, we can make effortless, inspired connections with other people, whether we are gregarious or introverted. When we show up and stand as ourselves, confident in our passions, beliefs and ideals, people understand our meaning and purpose, as we have removed barriers to authentic communication.

When we are not comfortable with ourselves, our skin, we are holding people at arm's length and are scared to be known.

When being our authentic self, we can be in communion with others, which is something that's really, really special when you experience it.

Ifyouarecuriousaboutthis,Icanalsorecommendresearching the practice of 'circling', an authentic relating practice with others, which can help to build this competence.

35.

Understanding Your Beliefs

Our beliefs about ourselves can become our self-fulfilling prophecy.

If we have healthy and positive beliefs about ourselves, our competencies, and how others see and value us, we can have effective and fulfilling lives and careers.

On the other hand, unhelpful and negative beliefs that make us doubt our worth and ability can have the opposite effect of constraining us, stunting our growth and potential, so we never quite fully express our true talents and abilities. This can also cause others to doubt us, preventing, for example, that promotion or the next new client having faith in us.

When we are acting as our authentic selves, and we understand our personal brand and are resourced with a positive set of beliefs, we are expressing as our true selves. This triggers something called the Pygmalion Effect.

The Pygmalion Effect describes the situation where, when we hold positive views and beliefs, this in turn reflects how others perceive us in positive ways. This enhances our self-esteem and belief in our own efficacy, enabling us to take on greater challenges and achieve higher performance, creating a virtuous circle where our positive qualities are continually reinforced and enhanced. This enables us to grow, personally and professionally, and achieve our true potential and purpose in life.

Reflect upon your beliefs about yourself.

Is anything possible if you put your mind to it?

Or instead, do you believe others are born lucky, and life for you is a struggle?

Are you somewhere in-between?

We have beliefs about ourselves. Identify these and then combine them with the five words that you identified about yourself earlier in the book. Do your beliefs and your values align?

Our beliefs shape how we show up, and influence how we act towards others.

Many people have experienced the negative effect of the insecure leader, who believes knowledge is power, that their way is the right way and that employees must know their place. This belief comes from fear – a fear of a loss of power. So, the power held by such a leader is misused and has negative effects on the organisation and team. Such is the power of faulty beliefs to have a huge impact across a whole business.

Conversely, if your core value, aligned with your personal brand, is to be caring in your interaction with others, then your actions towards others will be sympathetic and compassionate. Your decisions will be just and wise. People will seek your counsel and seek to work with you and for you.

You will rise to a place of secure and authentic leadership in your role or community.

This will be because your actions towards others come from a place of love, compassion and caring for others. The way that you lead will show that you value your impact on others. Your congruence in action will ensure that the beliefs that others hold about you will align with your own values – that you are a loving, compassionate and caring person. This is how congruent personal brands are developed and recognised. It's not all about what you do; it is about how your actions and words are reflected and received by others.

Even better, the actions of others towards you are going to be as a loving, compassionate, caring and wise person who is accepted, and that is going to further reinforce your belief that you are a loving, compassionate and caring person, who acts with wisdom, expressing that in all aspects of your life, including your business or career.

Another example may be your belief about yourself that you take pride in being competent, focused and conscientious.

Your actions towards others will then reflect that by displaying high standards in all of your work and your interactions with others.

Others will begin to believe and recognise this. They will see, speak and share about you being competent. Their actions towards you will be the actions that they would make towards a competent person. That might be offers of work, promotions, speaking, networking, all of that good stuff.

As those actions and recognitions begin to make an impact on you. This reinforces your belief in the value of being competent, and so it becomes easy to make the effort to continue to be diligent and focused in your roles, inside and outside your career.

So, you can see that it's really important to have these positive beliefs about yourself. You must affirm and truly believe these positive strong messages and infuse them within your personal brand.

You must rediscover and recognise who you are to have absolute clarity in your personal brand.

You can then put that out into the world and attract the experiences that reinforce that and allow you to be in your fullest expression of yourself and your talents at this juncture of your life and beyond.

36.

Keeping Up Appearances

L et's think about what else can define your personal brand.

Your personal brand will be more recognisable if you also focus on your appearance and your signature style.

I had an excellent example of this from a colleague from my corporate career. It was a man I was working with, and part of his personal brand was his attention to detail and level of perfectionism.

This was reflected perfectly in the way that he was turned out.

The precise attention to detail with the shoes, the hair, the bespoke suit, the pocket square was elegant and artful. Absolutely everything about his appearance reflected who this individual was. Thankfully (and crucially) this was congruent with the quality of his work, so there was consistency and trust.

This meant I knew clearly how to communicate effectively with this individual, how to present ideas and what tasks he was best suited to as I delegated them.

Equally, I have brilliant academic colleagues that may have wild hair and eccentric colourful clothes. They are messy thinkers and non-linear. They are often highly creative. They are tangential thinkers and able to synthesise and put together novel theories and ideas. And their 'look' perfectly expresses that.

Your personal brand can also be evoked by your energy.

If your personal brand is around optimism, you need to be showing up as an optimistic person.

You don't want your social media, your Twitter posts, your Instagram or socials of choice to be a moan about the weather. Then I would know you are, in fact, not optimistic. It would be like having an unhappy happiness coach. It simply would not make sense.

Show up as who you are in all your engagements and in your energy.

It's also about your speech, it's about the messages you give, it's about what you say, it's about how you respond. It's your posture. The signifiers of your personal brand are pervasive – they are in everything you touch and every interaction.

If part of your personal brand is confidence, or boldness, be careful that this is reflected in your body language. If you walk into a room and avoid eye contact and hide in the corner, I'm not going to believe you are confident or bold.

It's good practice to be conscious and aware of your physicality. In meetings or events, do not use body language that shows you to be defensive or lacking energy.

When I coach clients in negotiation, the worst posture they can use is the 'folded arms'. When challenged, my clients think this posture makes them look tough, like a hardball negotiator. In fact, it says loudly, without words, "Impress me". This is a put-down to the other party, and if I am your other party, your pricing will have just increased by 20% for that disrespect, as this provokes confrontation instead of negotiation.

So, make sure that your posture is something that you check regularly.

Accept being videoed for analysis and feedback, however painful a process this may sound! Only by seeing yourself as others see you can you become self-aware of your quirks and habits. Question what you can control.

Remember, not all advice is good advice, as your body language needs to remain natural and congruent to you, not forced. An example is people being taught mirroring as a sales technique. If this technique is applied in a crude way, those taught this then simply copy the other person's every movement. Far from creating rapport, this brings about discomfort and even antagonism in the other person, seeing their every move being copied. This is very clearly the opposite of the result you wish to create.

If you are excitable and enthusiastic, do not accept the standard public speaking advice to limit the use of hand gestures. When public speaking, I frequently talk with my hands. For me, this is as natural as breathing and in my experience, it builds rapport with the audience as it is natural and congruent. It's part of my signature and who I am, and I acknowledge and embrace it. The one thing I have had to work on, however, is my pace of speaking when excited. I now consciously slow down my delivery, in a natural way, for non-native English speakers, as my clients are often international.

37.

Charisma

Your personal style and charisma are about bringing to the fore the flair and the flourish that you bring to things. Once you have defined your values and the other elements of your personal brand, and you are confident that these are reflected in your style, take what is great about you and amplify that tenfold.

Own it.

For example, my brand is **#GameChanger** – this is a bold and confident assertion about what I can help my clients to achieve. It's about daring to be different, putting great ideas together and innovating; it's about being unorthodox, maverick, fearless, and a bit left-field in your approaches.

This means that in leadership or strategy sessions, it is not unusual for me to have a conversation with corporate clients about intuition and energy, and about the need for meditation or spiritual practice in connection with finding purpose. Prior to working with me, many of my corporate clients may have thought this to be an unusual approach, and yet, time and again, client feedback is exceptional, as they find their eyes opened to a completely new way of looking at things.

I'll rock up comfortably to a client meeting in leopard-skin heels, red lipstick, a black dress and Chanel Number 5 if that is how I am feeling. It might be gold sparkles if it's a group training session or I am speaking on stage. Sometimes I do reflect and think I took one mentor's advice not to be a wallflower perhaps a little too literally!

A huge part of my brand is quick-thinking, irreverence and humour – I firmly believe if we can laugh at ourselves and bring lightness to serious topics like growing businesses, restructuring teams, and creating world-beating organisations and technological firsts, we can achieve our aims with ease. We must never get so caught up in our tasks and mission that we forget to be human.

Humanity is at the core of what I do, as my core purpose is to liberate people's potential. I'm always open to the 'how' that happens. Maybe my leaders create more jobs, creating the opportunity for others to express potential and talent; maybe I help my clients discover their voice and clarity of purpose. When what I am doing aligns, I am happy, and this shows in my work with clients and the ongoing relationships and successes that they can achieve.

Think about the examples I have given here – how do you dare to be different?

Where do you break the accepted norms?

How does your work stand out?

It may be in your written communications, or your design. It could be in absolutely anything. Bring your own sense of pizazz to your vocation, whatever that might be.

Your qualities are already defined and now it is time to add to this.

How do you put your unique stamp on things that make things uniquely yours?

Think about how you signal this to others.

For example, Robert Thompson, the furniture maker, would carve a mouse to distinguish his pieces – and this became a key part of his brand.

People buy into brands they can recognise.

The other famous mouse brand is Disney. Walt Disney's mission was to inspire his people to dream, believe, dare and do – expressed as 'The Disney Way'.

Laboutin shoes are instantly recognisable from their curve, height and the daring red of the sole. Women who choose to wear them are sending a signal that they are bold and confident women unafraid, like Ginger Rogers, to go backwards in high heels!

What's your Laboutin?

38.

Creating Your Connection to Your Brand

—————————————————

Once you have the words, phrases, visuals, slogans and styles that define your personal brand, it's now time to bring this all together.

Much like a vision board, take a cork board or a blank wall to create a visual representation of your personal brand and values. Get creative and turn your visuals and ideas into a picture or a collage. You could even use Pinterest.

What is key is that you create a visual way in which you can see daily your values, positive beliefs and qualities. This works as a form of positive affirmation practice. Your visual representation should, at a glance, encapsulate who you are and how you uniquely shine in the world.

Next, write your own personal brand statement.

This should bring together your positive qualities, values and beliefs, and your purpose, which you have hopefully discovered through reading this book and reflecting up to this point. This is not a one-off process; this is something to be repeated at regular intervals to keep checking your own alignment and refining your personal brand.

LAURA TRENDALL

To get started, I recommend you do a handwritten draft. Then go back, reflect, refine and perfect it. It will change periodically, as you find new passions and avenues and explore your possibilities and potential.

The prompts I would like you to capture now for your journaling over the week ahead as you develop and craft this statement are:

- what you're expert in
- the originality that you bring to projects
- the three best compliments you have received in your whole life.

Compliments are great, yet as women, all too often we can bat them away. We dismiss them and minimise them. We do not receive them gratefully and graciously.

If we can begin to receive these compliments, going back to the Pygmalion effect, this strengthens our understanding and reinforces our positive beliefs in ourselves. It makes it possible to stand in our power and act from our authentic self.

Think about what others see in you that you overlook. Your personal brand must be personal to you but if you are overlooking something important that everybody else sees about you, it may be that you're missing opportunities or not putting your message out in the clearest way to attract what you want.

A final word on personal branding is that question often asked by clients: "How much should I share of myself and my personal story?"

The answer is simple – it is however much you feel comfortable with, to remain in congruence.

Many people use storytelling to give examples of how their methods can overcome adversity, others remain deeply private and let their work speak for itself.

It really is a matter of **personal** choice, as it's **your** personal brand, and you own it.

Creating Your Powerful Network

39.

Why Are(n't) You Networking?

Networking is one of those skills that has come to prominence in the last 15 years or so, following the advent of LinkedIn.

Even though I headed a Women's Network in my corporate career, I'm not sure what we called networking before LinkedIn – maybe it was just going to a conference, for a coffee or down the pub. Networking, now though, even after the pandemic, is booming, both online and offline. There are groups and networks for all types of interests, industries and businesses, so there really is something for everybody.

So, why are you networking?

Is it because it's something that you've been told you should do, or ought to do?

To improve sales in your business?

Is it because you're looking for a new job and somebody has suggested that you need to network more?

Is it about creating opportunities?

Is it to build relationships with trusted connections?

Is it one or all of the above? Is it for some other reason?

Think about why you are networking. In fact, are you networking at all?

I have come across many clients who say, "I don't know how to network". Let's break that negative belief right here. In our everyday lives, we all network. We're always creating relationships with other people. We might recommend a great independent shop to a friend; we might connect another friend with the person that can help them with their CV or childcare, or with designing a logo. We network constantly, we just don't always recognise it as such.

Spend a moment just thinking about the connections you have made – your friends, your colleagues, your business buddies, your trusted mentors or confidantes.

Then think about the purpose of your relationships with those connections.

It's important to understand why you are networking and to reflect on what you may be looking for as you go about your daily life and make connections with people, either within or outside your organisation, and through the many other channels that are now available.

I have made many a great business contact on flights or at social events. I am that person that talks to people when travelling.

Understand both the purpose and the potential of your connections and build from the network you have already.

40.

What is a Network Anyway?

network is simply a group or system of interconnected people or things.

That's it. It's not complicated.

A Wheel Network is where a single main person is at the centre of that network, and everybody else has a relationship just with that person – there is no interdependency. An example might be a resource manager, allocating and directing work to a group of independent freelancers.

A Mastermind Group is an example of a free flow or star network, where everybody in the network is connected to everybody else. These are the sorts of networks we are seeing more and more, as people build alignments through interest groups. The network expands and grows as others are introduced through links and extensions of those networks.

Most networks are random and mixed, though to be part of a socially-based group may convey affiliation or trust depending on its purpose and whether it is a formal or informal grouping.

Networks can be formal, in the case of an organisation. If you're working for a company with a hierarchy, there will be a formal network, which is usually expressed via an organisational chart, showing the routes through which communications are supposed to happen.

There are also informal networks. You may have somebody that works in the Accounts Department who is a good friend and goes to lunch with somebody who's a manager within HR – those informal connections often allow people to be privy to information that doesn't follow the normal organisational flows.

41.

Map Your Network

Think about your personal and professional networks.

If you put yourself as a dot in the middle of a piece of paper, who is directly linked to you?

Who are you linked to through other people?

Which organisations are you linked to through other people?

Which communities of interest are you part of?

Begin to map out and understand who is within your network, the degree of closeness, the strength of the relationships, and the usefulness of these connections in your life and your career.

42.

Building Connections

network for me very simply equals connection.

It may be a large network of loose ties, or a small, focused network based on common causes and purpose.

When people say, "I can't network" or "I don't know how to network", and that may even be what you are saying to yourself right now as you read this, I will remind you that 'Networking' is simply about building connections with other people.

This is something we're naturally programmed to do as people and social beings. Even the most introverted can find a point of connection with others.

It is also helpful to think about where you network and, importantly, how you like to network and with whom.

I like to network with people with novel ideas, with shared meaning and purpose, and in nice surroundings, where we might share learning opportunities. My planned networking is mainly centred around membership clubs and organisations which fulfil my criteria and preferences.

My unplanned networking happens when travelling or at conferences by simply being open and curious.

43.

Be Open and Curious

Networking is not just about who you speak to within your organisation. It's not just about paid business networking. You can create networking opportunities anywhere if your eyes, ears and mind are open.

There are many different places where we come across many different people and I'm sure that you will have examples of seemingly random encounters which have become valued and trusted connections.

I'll give you just one example. Through Twitter, in 2011, I had somebody within my network who is now an associate that I do work with. I met this individual virtually as a connection through a random comment on an American colleague's tweet that they made. We began having a conversation through Twitter about common interests, which happened to be music. This was completely unrelated to business. We found out as we chatted that we had business interests and friends in common, and that led to meetings, conversations and opportunities for us to explore as collaborations.

You never know, when you make that initial connection with somebody, where the connection is going to lead.

I'm sure you all have examples where you have met somebody, perhaps in a social setting, when you find that you have something in common within your work field. Or you've met somebody through a project at work or education and find that there is a common social interest. Networks are built anywhere and everywhere that people meet and interact.

To network, sometimes all you need to do is go outside.

Networking is now a much more natural part of our lives, with social media and the rise of the internet, so use tools such as Twitter, Instagram, Facebook and LinkedIn to connect, both personally and professionally, with people across the globe with common interests.

44.

Golden Rules of Networking

_____

my first golden rule is to be open. By being open, I mean be who you are, be transparent, develop trust and create opportunities for others to contact you.

The second golden rule of networking is never to judge or make assumptions about the other person who you've met.

The best way to find out about somebody is to ask questions, and yet I've seen networking go so wrong, particularly within business networking. This usually happens when people make a snap judgement about the other person that they're networking with. This is usually when somebody assumes that somebody is either high status or low status.

Please don't put people into pigeonholes like that. Don't make assumptions about people. People can wrongly assume when networking that the person that they're talking to either has influence in an area that the person actually doesn't have influence over, or the other way round.

Some people assume the person in front of them is not important to talk to, usually on the basis of gender, accent, class or some other stereotype, and they then overlook that individual. You can observe these people looking over the shoulder of the person they are networking with and looking for the next person to move on to. What they may be missing, through arrogance or biased assumptions, is that the perfect contact they are seeking may be stood right in front of them. This happens when people lack genuine interest in people and when they don't ask engaging questions.

So, be curious and ask questions.

This brings us to the third golden rule – treat every person you meet as if they are the most important person in the world to you in that moment.

The fourth rule is to understand that networking is a bit like building a house. If you want to build a network with firm foundations, you need to build strong connections and develop rapport, and also sustain and develop each relationship. It's not simply about connecting and moving on.

45.

The Fortune in the Follow-Up

_____

I have now been networking formally, attending and speaking at events and informally networking socially, for a number of years, since the start of my professional life.

In that time, I have received SO many business cards. I would say that maybe 1 in 10 of those people made a connection in terms of being the first to initiate a further follow-up.

A lot of people will take your business card, take your contact information and then won't do anything with it in terms of developing a relationship.

The whole point of networking is to understand who you gel with and to create a relationship.

I watch people. I'll observe people at events doing their own version of speed networking, but in a less formal setting. They are running around the event trying to grab as many business cards as possible, thrusting theirs in the hands of anyone they can, regardless of interest or a connection being made. What they've neglected to do is to have a proper conversation with the people in front of them. That is a fundamental error.

They may leave the event with a pile of business cards, but because they haven't had a conversation, they have no detailed memory of who anyone is or how they might like to be approached. They haven't truly interacted with anyone and so they haven't built a connection or rapport or the beginnings of a relationship, with anyone in the room. What a wasted opportunity!

So, if you are going to formal networking events, just focus on making two or three quality connections. It's not about running around the room and spreading yourself thinly, it's about quality.

Once you have made some quality connections, follow up, and keep in contact. This may be something that you have committed to do between you, or it might involve following up informally. It may be making sure that you add somebody to your email list, that you give them a call, that you keep them in mind when you read a particular article that you think would be interesting to them. Whatever it is, ensure that you take some action to keep that connection alive.

46.

Loose Connections

_____

As our networks grow ever more and expand, it's important to maintain at least loose ties with people.

As an example, I had a lovely email from a former colleague recently. This colleague is somebody who I've known for over 20 years, from the beginning of my career. At times we had worked right next to each other and had been in the same team.

This was the first time I had heard from this colleague for about four years, and the reason I'd heard from them is that we have kept a loose tie through social media. It's a male ex-colleague and when I posted that I was running my GameChanger for Women programme, he took notice of this. He's a father to three daughters who are graduate professionals and he recommended that they come and speak to me about the programme.

This is somebody that I've known for 20 years. Because we've kept loosely in touch even after we've moved organisations, we have those loose ties and common connections, as well as trust from prior interactions and brand alignment.

We have had the odd conversation and exchanged the odd email,and this has now led to a positive outcome, both for his daughters and for me, because they are exactly the type of people that I love to work with.

So, maintain your networks, keep those loose ties there and remain visible.

47.

Listen Well

L isten carefully, as details matter – because people matter.

It's important, when you're connecting with people and continuing that relationship and those conversations, that you are able to recall details about what's going on for them.

Again, this is where loose ties and social media come into play.

We used to have a Rolodex or a little black book with all our network's details, but now we have social media. Pick up details about people's likes and dislikes, common interests, their personal stories, all those things people talk about on social media (which previously you would never be able to find out about), and make a note of these. It's these details which matter, beyond just the basic contact information, such as where somebody is working. It's about remembering their personal stories.

It may be remembering that somebody has a specific interest or hobby, or is working with a particular cause, or has had a particular family event. People don't just want to be seen in a one-dimensional way where it's just about the business relationship. We are much more satisfied when we feel truly seen.

Even in the workplace, there is more talk about authenticity, bringing the 'whole self' into your vocation.

People want to be seen and valued for being the individuals that they are.

So, details matter.

48.

It's Not About You

Be genuinely interested in the other person when you are having a conversation.

If you are genuinely interested, in your initial conversation, and in many of your follow-up conversations, it should never be about you. It's about the other person and the relationship.

By being genuinely interested, if you are networking because you're looking for job opportunities or sales, you can understand the market better. In turn, this adds value to you.

You can serve your connections and clients better when you listen with full presence and attention.

In any industry, it is not about the product that you're pushing, it's about the benefit to the people who are going to use your product, that need your product. It's about how you serve. So, it's always about the other person.

Likewise, if you're networking to find an opportunity for a new role in an organisation, it's about what that organisation is looking for and whether can you fulfil and meet that need through service.

Understanding more about what's going on outside of you than what's going on inside of you, through attentive listening, is a powerful networking tool.

Most people listen either to make a judgment or to respond, or they're thinking of the next question before the other person has even finished speaking. That is not really listening.

Deep listening is where you are paying full and present attention to the other person.

49.

Be Discerning

Curate and protect your network.

Think of your network as outer circles through to inner circles. As people begin to become closer to you, here are two critical things to do:

1. Conduct formal due diligence to check out credentials
2. Trust your intuition

Intuition is a powerful thing and sometimes your intuition will warn you that somebody is not a good fit for your network, and I had an experience with this many years ago.

Somebody approached me and my antenna was up. My instinct was, "No, don't go there, don't engage with this individual."

On the other hand, the introduction had come via a professional colleague in a regarded organisation, so I wrongly assumed that due diligence had already been done on this person.

Many people were telling me this person had a good network, it was a good opportunity, when I sounded them out for a second opinion.

Subsequently, it turned out that the opportunity and investment were not as presented. The costs of getting involved professionally with this person were far-reaching – a damaging financial hit, time and money spent on a legal case, and the impact of all the stress and anxiety on my health during pregnancy.

I wish I had chosen to listen to my instinct and my intuition. Beyond that, I should have conducted some detailed, factual due diligence on the individual concerned, as I probably would have discovered the trail of creditors in her wake and a string of financial and company failures.

The worst of the situation was that this whole episode had the potential to damage relationships in my network.

Thankfully, it didn't, because through my investment personally into my networking over time, I have built strong and solid bonds of trust with people. My network was resilient enough to be able to withstand the impact that this individual was potentially able to have on my business, and we have lived to see another day, a great deal wiser as a result.

I am very grateful that my business is still here, despite the individual trying to ruin my reputation.

Through my openness about the situation and pursuing legal remedies to a successful conclusion, this demonstrated my integrity to my network and helped me continue to find and work with the right clients.

The final word is to be very, very careful about who you bring into your network. In an age of fake news and scams, this can be difficult, as we increasingly rely on social media and the so-called social proof this confers on individuals.

Take time to build relationships, even where this happens in a virtual space. So many relationships are now built with no face-to-face contact. If you can't look someone in the eye in person, it can be difficult to read whether they are being truthful and acting with integrity.

If your intuition or instinct is telling you it's not a good fit, don't be afraid to walk away.

There seem to be many people within the personal development industry at the moment who say, "Take the opportunities, say yes and work it out later". You need to resist this. It is a form of manipulation, designed to make you feel you are at fault, to drive you in the direction of the other person's agenda.

If it's your network, if it's your brand, if it's your reputation, I urge you, be discerning.

From my own, sometimes painful, experience, I know that this is the right thing to do. I would rather keep my networks small and selective, particularly for my inner circle, than widely dispersed.

50.

Be Specific

_____

Know who and know what you are looking for.

This is because there is a law of reciprocity in networking – quite often what I need to know when I'm speaking with a contact is how I can help them.

What are they looking for?

I may not have an opportunity for that individual or I may not have the perfect connection today but given how widely I do network and the conversations that I have with people, you never know when the right opportunity may arise.

There may be two people you know that need to be matched, one for what the other one needs. Be that useful connector by being specific with your requests and your questions.

We see this happen daily on social media, and I do think women are exceptionally good at this skill of connecting others, without an agenda.

If you can articulate who and what you are looking for in a way that is simple to grasp for the other person, that can be an incredibly powerful tool to advance you.

51.

Give Without Agenda or Expectation

B e genuinely generous. Give without expectation.

Not everything you do for somebody is going to be recognised.

Sometimes you will not even be thanked – that is okay. Just do the right thing anyway as this is one of those things that reputations are built upon.

Knowing that you do the right thing, knowing that you work with integrity, knowing that you are able to put people together to make a difference, to make the connection, to advance everybody, is reward itself.

Everybody is going to have different successes and that's absolutely fine. Be generous.

'What is for you, will not go past you' is one of my favourite sayings.

There is no harm in introducing people. Even if you think they work in the same field as you, which is common in the consulting, training and coaching communities I am part of, as a lot of people work in what appear to be similar fields, yet they all approach things differently. Each has their own brand of magic and personal style.

Introduce people because there may be the right synergy – it's better that the right person gets the job than the wrong person gets the job, because you have chosen not to pass on that connection.

Do what you can genuinely and willingly. It is perfectly OK to put other people first, so don't be too concerned about it. Do it and then let it go.

52.

Don't Be a Wallflower

Recapping on the work we have reflected on earlier in the process, in the personal branding section, there are two principles to take away and apply:

1. **Be memorable by having a recognisable image**
    That might mean that you present a consistent image across social media. It may mean that you are recognisable to people through having a distinctive and memorable personal brand and style when you meet your network in person.

2. **Be congruent and be yourself**
    Make sure you can clearly and confidently articulate what you do, and what your unique point of value is, so that when opportunities come up, your network are able to think, "Aha, that's the person that does that thing" and make that connection for you.

53.

Keep In Touch

One challenge in effective networking is to manage and maintain relationships with outer circle connections – those people who are not that close to you right now.

Do be aware that people can move in and out of the circles of connection throughout the duration of your relationship with them.

It's simplest to keep in touch with your outer circle through social media as a minimum, maybe through a broadcast strategy. Updates and a message here and there are fine.

For closer connections or those who've opted into it, email is a great way to stay in touch. Use email for sending out a regular newsletter, which is an important tool, but also use one-to-one emails as well.

Make sure you are personalising where there is something particularly relevant. One of the things that I do which is brilliant for getting back in touch with people within my network who I wanted to re-engage with, over the Christmas or other holiday periods, is to send each of them a personalised email.

I am also a firm advocate for making phone calls. Many people rely on messages, but nothing replaces the direct connection of a phone call. Where you have a strong enough relationship with somebody, diary in time for a call every month or two. And then progress to in-person meetings.

For me, it's important to make the time to meet as many of my contacts in person as possible. So, I often let people know ahead if I am in a particular area or I'm going to give talks somewhere local to them. I then try and make some sort of space available to make a reservation, whether that's for lunch or dinner or drinks and use that opportunity before or after the event that I'm speaking at or attending to make connections with people in person.

I think it's so important to give people the opportunity to come and speak to you in person.

If you're somebody that they have followed on social media for a while, and you're going to be in a particular town, drop a few select personalised messages to people you'd like to understand better to come and connect.

So, take the time to do this.

We have the tools available, more powerful tools than we've ever had. So, use them.

54.

Keep It Relevant

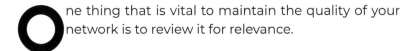

One thing that is vital to maintain the quality of your network is to review it for relevance.

I regularly download my different social media lists and go through each one. I then look at when I have last contacted each person and by what method.

Are they personally known to me?

Is it too long since we've had a conversation, do we need to reconnect?

Are they still relevant in terms of where they are sitting now, are they in a career that is related, have they moved into a field that I know something about or could be able to help them with?

If that's the case, I'll get in touch and I'll make that offer of help if that's what needed.

So, always make sure that you are reviewing your network for relevance.

Other things that you want to consider when you're reviewing your network are listed here:

- How frequent is your contact with this individual?
- What is the usual method of contact and do you now need to switch it up a bit?
- If you've always corresponded via email and you're now thinking, "We've got something in common here, they're working on this project, I'm working on something similar", get in touch and suggest a phone call. Switch it up.
- If there's somebody that you've known quite well from a long time ago, is that somebody that's still in alignment with you and with your values?
- Do you still really want to keep them within your network, or do you want to be selective and move them to one of the outer circle spaces for the time being?
- Do you have a common area of interest?
- If you need to re-connect with someone, reach out personally. Whether it's through commenting on social media or sending them a direct message, whether it's a personal email or picking up the phone and inviting them for lunch; you'll know what the right thing is to do to re-establish your connection.

Keep your network warm.

Action and Accountability

55.

Identify Your Actions

What do you do when your to-do list is crazy?

The first thing is to go through it and understand exactly what you need to do.

Spend the time to make a detailed list, regardless of whether the task or niggle is large or small, trivial or important. Pick a time when you're not going to be interrupted, when the phone won't be ringing off the hook.

In my world, a great time to do this is Sunday afternoon.

There are many different methods that you can use for this. Some people prefer to create a handwritten list, some prefer to key it into their smartphone, or put it straight into a document that they can work from.

The thing to consider when you are getting it all down is to look at all the different places where these actions have come in from.

What channels are all these demands coming from?

Are they from emails, which ones are family and social, are some through social media? Are some even from the old-fashioned way, through the post?

When all these things filling your in-tray come in, where and how are they reaching you? What are the different at which you receive the incoming request? Back in the old days we used to have in-trays, now we have so many different places where people can make contact with us that it can be hard to keep track, and so limiting some methods might be necessary.

Identify where you're being contacted, where your requests to be actioned are coming from.

This will allow you to create systems for when, where and how you set your times to allocate and respond, and what expectations you communicate through those different channels.

What I'd also like you to consider when you do that is whether these are internal demands, i.e. self-driven, the obligations that you are creating for yourself.

Through the actions that you're taking, the things that you're committing to through your life, you set your priorities.

Are they external demands, coming from other people's requests and agendas?

If the demands are external, are they in alignment with the vision that you hold for yourself?

Are the actions required in alignment with what you've identified as your core purpose?

Is it something that you need to do because there's a requirement for it from a regulatory or legal viewpoint?

Is it something that you feel that you need to do because other people's wants/wishes are influencing you?

Really begin to understand what's driving the actions that you're being asked to complete.

If you do have a heavy 'to-do' list, understanding that, and deciding whether those requests on your time are valid, is an important and useful start point to conquering that list.

56.

Manage Your To-Do List

_____

We've talked about different ways you may identify and capture your to-do list.

Lists can be great – they work well for many people. You may prefer to use a spreadsheet.

Part of my background is project management, and I find spreadsheets are highly effective because I can categorise things into the types of tasks that they are, and what the outcomes are going to be.

With my actions, I tend to quantify each task in terms of what the value is going to be – both financially and in terms of supporting my goals.

Other ways that you may choose to identify and allocate your tasks is through diarising each task in a time block in your calendar or using index cards.

Index cards can be powerful and flexible when you're going through a planning and mapping phase for the launch of a project or plan, because you can group tasks together, re-order them and then move things around and look at how you re-prioritise.

Index cards are a useful way of dealing with priorities on a daily basis as well, if you like variety. Simply pick three things that need to be done from your stack that are not time constrained, or that you are drawn to, and work through them as fast as you can. This is another great hack for building your self-efficacy.

57.

Prioritise

_____

When you're setting your priorities, think about the request that you've received or the action that you need to take.

Firstly, is it important and secondly, is it urgent?

Further qualifiers that I would add to the importance and urgency criteria are:

- Who is it important to?
- Who is it urgent for?
- Why is it either important or urgent?
- What is the long-term impact of this action being completed or uncompleted?

Considering these impacts can guide you in how you prioritise your tasks.

This allows you to see clearly what really needs to be done first.

You can also evaluate what you can schedule to better or more convenient times.

You can be flexible around other priorities that you have or the things that may be more urgent due to changes. You can determine when is the best time to undertake a task resulting from the flow and dependency of another project or knowing when people are going to be available for what you need.

Always ask yourself – does the activity align with your core purpose?

That is really the primary factor to think about when you are scheduling in your tasks. If it does not align, why is it on your list?

58.

Effective Scheduling and Planning

In the GameChanger method, the core purpose is the foundation that everything should flow from.

I use diaries and calendars when I'm scheduling so that I can look at the whole year from the perspective of my core purpose. Here are the 7 steps that take in my own GameChanger process, and these are ones which I recommend you adopt.

1. I define the core purpose for the year and expand on my vision for the year ahead.
2. This enables me to set the supporting annual objectives I need to meet to move my business and life from A to B. There is always a start point and an end point, to measure progress clearly.
3. I break my big vision down and plan out what my monthly goals are going to be for each month of the year, ensuring each goal or performance objective links back to the core purpose and annual goals.
4. This sets out a clear plan of what needs to be achieved each month. Typically, that involves 3 to 5 key goals

that go into my system for action, measurement and attention on the first day of each month.

5. The plan is set down in my calendar and my goals are committed to, in writing. This gives me a benchmark to review my achievement against as we progress through the year.

6. From the monthly goals, I develop a weekly checklist of the sub-tasks.

7. Finally, I layer into the schedule my regular tasks, the things that I do week in, week out, plus the additional tasks that may arise, that support me towards both my monthly goals and achieving my vision and core purpose.

Think about this process and then apply it to your own circumstances.

It may be that you are spending time writing up reports on a Monday; it may be that you're focusing on marketing and sales calls on a Tuesday; or it may be you act towards your fitness goals and play tennis on a Friday.

This will create a weekly checklist of things to do. As far as you can, standardise and make this a regular routine. This makes non-standard tasks much easier to slot into your diary and work around if everything else is running like clockwork.

The next level is to dive down into your daily planner. This should set out by each hour what you plan to do, any appointments, any family commitments or chores and any health matters.

Some people prefer to have this in a paper diary. I am an Outlook girl and don't see that changing, as I like the reminders that sync to my other technology, like my phone and devices.

I like the fact that I can see at a glance exactly what I should be doing on any given day and that works highly effectively for me.

So, make sure that whatever system you choose works for you – just make sure that it is a system that you are comfortable working with, as that will mean you will be happy to use it consistently over a sustained period of time.

Experiment with different methods and find a system that works for you.

59.

Automate!

---

useful way to manage my client time is to use online booking.

If people want to meet with me or want to have a phone call, rather than playing phone tag or email tag, depending on the individual, I can direct them to an online booking link.

My client can choose a time that works for them and works for me.

60.

Zone Your Time

A technique which I have found works well for me in terms of planning efficient use of my time, is to have different 'zones' of time for work, family, travel, health, hobbies, learning and development, networking, and social activities.

Sunday evenings for me are synonymous with planning. It's rare that a Sunday evening does not involve me sitting down and looking through what's coming up for the week ahead.

I have specific days set aside for client calls.

I have days earmarked for travelling and seeing clients or networking activities or speaking engagements.

I have other days which are specifically for administration, and for strategic thinking.

By having this regular plan that I work to, I know that on a Monday I'm with clients. If you ask me for a call, then I'm generally going to be available after 3pm. Create a schedule and a rhythm to your week that works for you.

61.

Keep the Rhythm

_____

If you really don't know where you're starting from, or where your rhythm is in your week, conduct a study for two weeks and evaluate your time.

Evaluate where you're spending it and how well that's working for you.

Map out visually on a weekly chart what your ideal week would look like. Begin to think about what could work better for you.

In our household, we have specific days when certain household tasks are completed.

Everybody knows where they're at with things, and chores always get completed, which leads to a calm, healthy and productive environment.

We know as a family that there are certain things that we do for relaxation over the weekend, and we have those times together. Those times are kept sacrosanct in our family, and it works well for us.

62.

Choose the Best Person for the Task

Review the actions that you are taking. One thing that we sometimes overlook is whether we are the best person for the job. This may be as a result of a perception about our seniority or skills, or for some other reason.

Think whether there are areas or tasks on which you are spending time that may be playing to your weaknesses, rather than your strengths. These should be delegated.

Create opportunities to collaborate with others. Recruit other people either into your team or into your organisation to support you. Promote growth.

For example, think about balancing your team with complementary skills:

You may be a GameChanger (obviously this is my area of interest), someone capable of seeing the future and looking at how we need to change things, someone whose strengths lie in innovation and design. GameChangers can generate a lot of activity and for that we need to collaborate with implementers.

An implementer is someone who can provide you with complementary support by focusing on getting things done and ensuring more detailed tasks are completed, which can often be a weakness for a GameChanger.

This team could be strengthened with a third person, a strategist who is good at envisioning what needs to happen, and then planning the steps to be taken in the bigger journey towards your vision. Add their talent to the mix and the team is kept on track, driving the project to a successful outcome, on time and on budget.

It is a rare person that can perform each of these roles, so it is essential we pick the right team.

Think about where your zone of strength is. We all have things that we're stronger at, and we all have things that we need support with.

Looking at your strengths and weaknesses, are you the best person for what you're doing?

With so many different actions required for a project, are you understanding when to outsource and when to delegate tasks?

By assembling the right team, you free up your time to focus on your areas of expertise and achieve your tasks in a far more efficient manner.

63.

Outsourcing

---

ow do you know when to outsource? For me, that comes down to what I call the four 'E's.

1. Enjoyment
The task or action that you're being asked to look at – is it something that you enjoy? Are you naturally enthusiastic about it, as it plays to your strengths?

2. Efficiency
Are you efficient at it?

3. Effectiveness
Even if you may enjoy it immensely, are you effective at achieving the task or action?

4. Earning potential
All too often, I see people taking on tasks below their pay grade, and in doing so they are eroding their earning potential as they are tasks an assistant could do at lower cost. We should focus on doing the tasks where we add value and get rewarded.

A common trap you may get caught in is posting on social media. So many people spend time doing this, pushing their marketing uphill themselves when it's often more efficient and effective to outsource or automate social media posting.

So, think about what you spend your time on in your career or in your business and be clear on the opportunity cost of choosing not to outsource some of those activities.

You can also think about the opportunity cost of not outsourcing things at home like domestic tasks, gardening and odd jobs.

These things can cause massive stress and conflict within a household.

I coached a group of high-performing men and seeing the lightbulb go on for them was a revelation. I suggested that if they outsourced doing the jobs that they hated around the garden and home, they could do the things that were important like spending more quality time with their family.

So, it's not just about financial cost – it's also about the health cost, the positive benefits that we can get from choosing one task or action over another and being selective about what we do.

Of course, when outsourcing any sort of action or activity it's critical to find the right supplier.

What you do not want to do is work with somebody who is going to cause a problem or not do something to your satisfaction. That generates even more stress when we should be minimising it and working towards positive outcomes. Take the time to get solid recommendations and find the right supplier for you. Understand what you're asking them for.

64.

Delegating and Outsourcing

When delegating and outsourcing go wrong, it usually goes wrong because the delegation is poor.

It is never entirely the fault of the other party or supplier, or whoever it has been delegated to. It is normally bad communication and poor instructions by the person making the delegation or outsource brief.

To delegate effectively, you need to identify precisely what it is you need to delegate.

You need to plan what you're going to delegate, with clear timescales, and communicate that expectation.

Create a clear brief.

You may even create a Standard Operating Procedure.

For example, how would you outsource your sales activity? Your sales pipeline is crucial to the success of your business so it's vital that you describe exactly the sales process you need to an outsourced agent.

Describe in detail what the qualification part of the sales process includes.

Be clear on what qualification information you want them to collect.

Be clear on how many days after doing X (if X isn't delivering results) they need to move onto an alternative strategy and what steps need to be taken to agree this.

So, invest time upfront in being organised, creating a detailed brief which defines in detail all the processes required which you are delegating or outsourcing. Be clear to what standard you require tasks to be competed, with checklists, examples, forms and targets.

65.

Success Comes From Review

Review is critical during any project or tasks.

You need to keep an ongoing review in place, particularly if something is part of a longer-term plan towards your vision, mission and goals. At the end of each project or sprint, conduct a final review and give feedback if working with others. Self-evaluate your own work.

Think about what went well.

Identify what can be improved.

The important thing to remember about giving feedback in the review process is that it does need to be two-way. Two-way dialogue is not a one-way monologue.

66.

Accountability and Stakeholders

Identify your accountability dream team.

Who do you need around you, to run ideas by after you have conducted all the planning and scheduling, to help you to achieve what you're doing?

Share your deadlines and goals and be willing to be held accountable.

Additionally, there are four stakeholders where you owe accountability:

- Customers (internal and external)
- Suppliers and partners
- Assistants and employees
- Mentors, coaches and accountability partners

Customers are clearly part of accountability and internal customers are just as important within your organisation as your external customers. Through customer feedback, such as surveys and meaningful dialogue, we understand how well we're performing and delivering in the actions and tasks that we set.

How close are we to meeting the needs of our clients?

How well we are doing against the market?

We may receive this information via different routes of feedback. This feedback is probably one of the things that's going to be most helpful to you in your career growth or in your business journey.

We usually have suppliers and one thing that often surprises me is the answer to this question:

"Do you hold regular reviews on the effectiveness of your relationships with suppliers?"

Most people do not do this regularly, if at all. Many people engage a supplier and then choose to let that relationship continue because they think it's going to be too difficult to change, or they don't want to confront a particular issue, and so they avoid communicating with them.

Good relationships with suppliers can be so positive and a source of innovation, and can help you to be more accountable in your business, because you choose to work with that supplier in partnership. Your success depends not just on how they supply you, but how well you communicate with them as their client and what standards you hold your supplier accountable to.

For assistants and employees, processes should exist between you to ensure clear accountability and handovers.

Whether you are building your organisation virtually, whether you are part of a large corporate, or whether you have a team of people working for you, understand where your checkpoints are. Make sure that everything is clear, and that people know when things pass from one person to the next.

Define who is responsible, who is accountable and how those confirmations are going to check that something has been done and completed to a satisfactory level.

It's not about just what we communicate – it is very much how and when we communicate.

With accountability in organisations, when it goes wrong, usually somebody's done what they needed to do, but they have not communicated it. It's not seen, it's not heard, it's not understood by the other people who are relying on them.

My experience working with large organisations was that when things didn't go right for a team or project, it was down to failures in communication.

Be clear how and when tasks should be done and be proactive in your communication.

Finally, accountability partners are a valuable addition to any support network. Accountability partners can be formal in terms of having a coach or mentor, or can be an informal arrangement where two peers that work together agree to hold each other accountable on a regular basis for what they want to achieve.

It can be an informal buddying scheme.

What's really important about accountability partners is that they're well matched, in terms of understanding and education and seniority. It's important that they have a balance of skills between them. It's a reciprocal relationship where both partners should get equal positive value.

There must be reciprocity and a reason for the accountability relationship.

In the case of buddying, it must be a fair exchange with equal time listening and receiving.

Final Words

This book has been written with the intention of simplifying and sharing accessible tools and strategies to help any woman at any stage of her career or business life to become more successful.

We all deserve to be fulfilled and to live a life where we are supported to reach our full potential.

My hope is that you can take something from this book that changes something personally and positively for you, whether it is becoming more organised, being the person you wanted to become, or taking the leap to try something new.

You define what success is for you, and what a #GameChanger would be for you.

If you make great progress from anything I have shared here, I'd love to hear about your success stories, and connect further through the #GameChanger community.

You are warmly invited to join us at www.gamechanger.vip/community.

Wishing you success, happiness and a bright future,
Laura

Join Us in the GameChanger for Women Community

The GameChanger for Women community is specifically for women in business, with a simple but ambitious objective:

> We strive to help to create women leaders in business. We work with women who want to step up and make an impact in their communities and for the future. GameChanger exists to empower and change lives.

Now that you have this book, we'd love you to join us. Just visit www.gamechanger.vip/community where you can find out more information.

About the Author

Most of my early career was in the technology sector, at corporate giant BT. The reason I originally went into that corporate career, and focused on strategy, sales, finance and negotiation is because I knew that I wanted to be successful in business, and that this, for me, was the route to making a difference.

The late '90s and early 2000s were a time of great opportunity in the fast-growing tech sector, but there were few female leaders in tech, enabling me to make my mark. I became involved with women's networks, coaching and mentoring others throughout my career before professionally qualifying as a coach in 2008, when I was expecting my first daughter.

I'll admit, my own career has been far from traditional – starting with being a bit of a rebel and leaving home at 16 to forge my own way ahead. For that, I'd like to thank my parents for teaching me to stand on my own two feet to become the independent and resourceful woman I am today. I still had the prospect of a traditional path ahead of me after an offer from one of the top law schools in the country but was drawn to join the world of work instead, out of necessity.

I kept going, and finally got to the first round of attending university. That time, I found myself getting into a debate about ethics, and the politics of law. The rebel and the changemaker in me could not simply be quiet, and the views held by the faculty and the conformist nature of the environment made me decide yet again to leave the traditional path, to study fashion and business.

At the tender age of 20, I was given the opportunity to join a rapidly growing mobile technology company in the glamorous city of Leeds – well, they had Harvey Nichols, so if you came from the north of England in the 90s, that was truly cosmopolitan and glamorous, in the days before super-brands.

I could see the potential in the emerging technology markets and the opportunity of city life, so I put the fashion plans on hold, with the intention of focusing on learning all that I could about marketing and planning to return to my two great loves of fashion and music once I had acquired more real business experience. I joined the Women's Network on my first day in BT, as I really felt the need for more female business leaders and that this would be a great place to meet likeminded women.

Having negotiated access to a degree-level course while serving my apprenticeship, it became clear big changes were about to happen in the company I was working in. I discovered that this meant that the promotion I had been working so hard to secure was now off the table. So, instinct told me to **play a bigger game**.

My discipline and focus, combined with my love of strategy and growing businesses ensured success as I moved to London at the dawn of the millennium for my next promotion.

Back at the turn of the millennium, I also sought a coach to help me make the next jump to a management role and focused on what my marketable talents were to the global part of the company I worked for. I knew my ambitions lay in working internationally and meeting others from many cultures. I put in the hours and did the research and applied for jobs far above my age and experience.

Guess what? It paid off. My ability to showcase my talents, to see the future and be open to possibilities impressed my interviewer so much that I did **not** get the job I interviewed for. How can that be a success, I hear you thinking... let me share this with you:

Within 30 minutes of leaving the interview, I had a job offer for a newly created role, at a better grade and salary, that matched my skills and aspirations, with huge potential to progress my career. It was a risk. I wasn't qualified. It was uncharted territory. It required a complete relocation. And I was required to start in 2 weeks. Instinct kicked in and pushed the fears out of my head, as I heard myself saying, "Why not? Let's go for it."

I know that there is much that I have been prepared to do in my career, which went against the grain, and certain qualities which I have nurtured and cultivated. All of these have contributed to my success:

- my first £10M sale at the age of 23
- rapid promotions
- chairing a 2000-strong network by the age of 35

- becoming the go-to expert on increasing profitability and business strategies for growth
- coaching over 1000 senior leaders in 29+ counties from over 50 nationalities
- and finally, a happy and balanced home life raising my 3 beautiful daughters to be empowered young women of the future.

I continue to run my own consultancy, and travel internationally sharing my knowledge, and have now started a publishing company.

I translated that passion from initially working in the technology industry, in male dominated environments, to using technology and the power of the internet for myself, to connect with people globally and to work with growing businesses, as well as more established businesses, on communication, change management and leadership.

From this deep expertise and vantage point, I created **GameChanger for Women**. This was based on my experiences as a coach and mentor, and chairing the Women's Network within BT plc. I was privileged to coach a number of our business leaders and interview senior women. I began to understand, apart from my own experience, what the common experiences of women were that occasionally held them back. What keeps us awake at night. Where our passions lie. The regrets held for roads not taken. And where we find challenge, counterbalanced with courage and persistence, within our businesses and within our career lives.

The other great contributor to my success was the advice and mentoring I received in my career from many colleagues, from all levels – learning to listen to the wisdom of others and receive this gratefully.

The ability to approach challenges with an open mind has served me well, and I enjoy constructive and creative relationships with my fellow business owners and professional associates.

That said, I could count on one hand the women that were known to me in my corporate career who were more senior, and they were often so busy back then as to be unapproachable. This was back in the age of the stereotypical power-suited female boss, feared by all men who worked for her. There were a couple of notable exceptions though in my early career, who inspired my progression to eventually stand for, and lead one of the most influential networks for women in technology and synthesise my learning from that time into **GameChanger for Women**.

The last 10 years have seen remarkable progress in female leadership, with women supporting women and breaking the glass ceilings of power and income, truly shaping their own destinies, for themselves and their loved ones, all at a much faster rate than ever before. This has been accelerated with the democratisation and access to technology, changes in work styles and the pioneers who show on social media that this can be done, inspiring women of all generations and backgrounds.

With all these tools at your disposal, and the support of the community (www.gamechanger.vip/community), I look forward to hearing about your success!